EXTREMISTS

CJ Hopkins

BROADWAY PLAY PUBLISHING INC
224 E 62nd St, NY NY 10065-8201
212 772-8334 fax: 212 772-8358
BroadwayPlayPubl.com

THE EXTREMISTS
© Copyright 2010 by CJ Hopkins

First printing: November 2010
I S B N: 978-0-88145-441-3
Book design: Marie Donovan
Typographic controls & page make-up: Adobe InDesign
Typeface: Palatino
Printed and bound in the U S A

ABOUT THE AUTHOR

CJ Hopkins is an expatriate American playwright, and occasional stage director, based in Berlin. His early plays and experimental stage-texts were first produced during the 1990s in New York City by HERE Arts Center, The Present Company, Monkey Wrench Theater, Soho Think Tank/Ohio Theater, Manhattan Theater Source, and the Knitting Factory, among other companies, and regionally by Amaryllis Theater, Philadelphia, and Alchymia Theater, Chicago. While in New York, Hopkins received playwriting fellowships from the Drama League of New York and Jerome Foundation and was a 1995 Resident Artist at Mabou Mines/Suite. In 2002, the U K premiere of Hopkins' best-known play, HORSE COUNTRY, was presented at the Edinburgh Fringe Festival. The production, directed by John Clancy, received universal acclaim and won several awards including a Scotsman "Fringe First" for new writing, and, ultimately, the most prestigious writing award of the Festival, the Scotsman "First of the Fringe Firsts". HORSE COUNTRY went on to tour and be produced internationally, and was published by Methuen Drama in 2004. In 2005, the world premiere of Hopkins' SCREWMACHINE/ EYECANDY, OR: HOW I LEARNED TO STOP WORRYING AND LOVE BIG BOB was produced at the Edinburgh Fringe Festival by Scamp Theatre Ltd. The production, again directed by Clancy, received broad critical acclaim, and Hopkins was awarded his second Scotsman 'Fringe First' for innovation and outstanding new writing. The U S premiere of SCREWMACHINE/EYECANDY followed in 2006, at 59E59 Theaters, and the play was published in 2007 by Broadway Play Publishing Inc. Since 2007 Hopkins has received further play and video commissions, in both English and German, including a 2006 site-specific piece commissioned by the Freie Universität Berlin and performed in the Norman Foster-designed FU Philological Library, the "Berlin Brain", and the 2009 commission of THE EXTREMISTS by 7 Stages. CJ Hopkins is represented by Ronald Gwiazda, Abrams Artists Agency, New York.

THE EXTREMISTS was commissioned by 7 Stages, Atlanta. The world premiere was produced by 7 Stages, English Theatre Berlin and PushPush Theater at F40, Berlin, in February 2009. The cast and creative team were as follows:

NORMAN KRIEGER..Del Hamilton
DICK HEDGEROW... Tim Habeger

Director.. Walter D Asmus
Stage manager.. Shelby Hofer
Assistant stage manager ....Katie Pfohl
Set & costumes...Faye Allen
Lighting Design ....Ralf Arndt

The U S A premiere was produced by 7 Stages, Atlanta, in March/April 2009. The cast and creative team were as follows:

NORMAN KRIEGER..Del Hamilton
DICK HEDGEROW... Tim Habeger

Director.. Walter D Asmus
Stage manager...Heidi S Howard
Set & costumes...Faye Allen
Lighting design ....Jessica Coale

CHARACTERS & SETTING

NORMAN KRIEGER, *a poetic terrorist, posing as an anti-terrorism expert*

DICK HEDGEROW, *another poetic terrorist, posing as a T V journalist*

Whatever THE EXTREMISTS is, it is certainly not a representational drama. Formally, it is more akin to vaudeville than anything resembling naturalism. Most of the dialog should be delivered straight out, into the house, in the direction of the spectators, but not directly to the spectators, at least not until the final few minutes.

THE EXTREMISTS is to be performed with no intermission. No late seating should be allowed.

ACKNOWLEDGMENTS

Thanks to Del Hamilton, Walter D Asmus, Tim
Habeger, Faye Allen, Shelby Hofer, Günther Grosser,
Bernd Hoffmeister, Ralf Arndt, Katie Pfohl, Sydney
Ellis, Heidi Howard, Antje Grabenhorst, Inka-Charlotte
Palm, Russ Vick, Peter Ehrentraut, Eva van Dok, Fred
Backus, Dan Hope, Jason Howard, Manhattan Theatre
Source, Nicole Poole, Dan Berkey, Julia Lee Barclay,
Josh Taylor, Goethe Zentrum Atlanta, Helena Prince,
Clayton Nemrow, Julia Horvath, Jeffrey Mittleman,
Jean-Theo Jost, Andy Snelling, Ron Gwiazda, Amy
Wagner, Martin Denton, Julie Blumenthal, Thomas
Diecks

DICK: Good evening, and welcome to Issues in Focus.
I'm Dick Hedgerow, your host, in Washington.
Tonight we're devoting the entire program
to an in-depth discussion of the threat of extremism,
both here, at home, and throughout the world.
To help us do that, we have with us tonight
one of the foremost experts in the field,
Norman Krieger, a senior analyst
and co-founder of the Center for Advanced Strategic
   Studies.
In addition to his work at the CASS,
Mister Krieger is the author of the recent best-seller,
Extremism in the 21st Century and Beyond.
Mister Krieger, welcome to Issues in Focus.

NORM: Call me Norm, Dick. Pleasure to be here.

DICK:
Your book is focused on the psychology, is it not?
The extremist mindset?

NORM: That's right, Dick.

DICK: Their psychological motivation.
What they want. What makes them tick.

NORM: That, yes, and how they spread their views.

DICK: Good. So let's set the scene a little, shall we?

NORM: Sure.

DICK: O K. So...here we are.

NORM: Yes.

DICK: Dawn of a new millennium.

NORM: Mm hmm...

DICK: Single super-power world.

NORM: Sure.

DICK: Communism...dead and buried.

NORM: Right.

DICK: Extremism...number one threat?
Number one threat the world is facing?

NORM: There is no greater threat, Dick.

DICK: In your book, you call it "the final threat".

NORM: It's going to be with us for some time to come.

DICK:
And we need to get used to living with the threat.
Get to know it. Understand it.

NORM: We don't really have much choice in the matter.

DICK: It's not going away.

NORM: No. It isn't.

DICK: The current threat level is orange, is it not?

NORM: Actually, I think it's yellow today.

DICK: Yellow? I'm sorry. I thought it was orange.

NORM: It's definitely one or the other, Dick.

DICK: Yellow or orange.

NORM: Unless something changed.

DICK: Which is possible, right?

NORM: Right. Sure.

DICK: In any event, the threat is still there.

NORM: We have to operate on that assumption, yes.

DICK: And what are we doing about the threat?

NORM: Well, Dick, we're doing all we possibly can.

DICK: Is it enough?

NORM: Well, it is and isn't.

DICK: Is and isn't.

NORM: That's right, Dick.
We can't eliminate the threat entirely.
But we can certainly do what we're doing, and then some.

DICK: To keep it to an acceptable level.

NORM: Exactly, Dick. A manageable level.
That's the goal we have to strive for.

DICK: Manageability.

NORM: Absolutely.
But look, having said that, I want to emphasize,
that any level is unacceptable.
The goal remains elimination.

DICK: Complete and total elimination.

NORM: Yes, but we have to be realistic.

DICK: About what's possible.

NORM: Achievable, right.
We don't want to foster a false sense of security
or sell anybody a bill of goods.
At the same time, we don't want to alarm the public
unnecessarily, unless we have to.

DICK: By painting the picture as scarier than it is.

NORM: We can't afford to let down our guard.
It's important that we all maintain our vigilance.
Just not to the point where it becomes disruptive
or changes how we live our lives.
We need people to go about their normal lives,
keeping in mind that the next attack
could happen anywhere at any time.

DICK: With no warning at all.

NORM: I'm afraid so, Dick.

DICK: So is there cause for heightened concern at the
   moment?

NORM:
I wouldn't want to frame it in exactly those words.
The threat is there. No question, it's there.
But to what degree on any given day—

DICK: We can't let the threat take over our lives,
is what you're saying.

NORM: That's what they want.

DICK: The extremists.

NORM: Right.

DICK: To scare us.

NORM: Yes.

DICK: To disrupt our lives. Make us feel vulnerable.
Out of control. Scared. Confused.
Which there's no cause to feel, is what you're saying.

NORM: No. On the contrary, if people understood
the level of surveillance and pre-emptive monitoring—

DICK: Of extremist groups?

NORM: It's around the clock.

DICK: I guess we don't hear about all the thwarted
   attacks.

NORM: Not all of them, no.

DICK: For security reasons.

NORM: A lot of these are ongoing operations.
But I can tell you this much. The number is high.

DICK: The number of thwarts.

NORM: We've thwarted a few.

DICK: Are we talking double digits?

NORM: I really can't comment.

DICK: But a meaningful number.

NORM: Definitely, Dick.
And when you add to that groups that may have just
    formed
or were only in the early conceptual stages—

DICK: Of planning an attack?

NORM: Potentially, yes.
Potentially planning. Or in the pre-planning phase.
Displaying tendencies in any event.

DICK: Tendencies.

NORM: Typical extremist tendencies.
Patterns. It's all about patterns of chatter.
Conversations. Words people use.

DICK: Profiling.

NORM: Yes. That, and surveillance.

DICK: Pre-emptive measures.

NORM: Wherever possible.
Look, what your viewers, and the public at large,
needs to understand and bear in mind
is the fluid and slippery nature of this threat
and thus, by extension, the nature of our response.

DICK: Which needs to be fluid as well, I take it.

NORM: It does, Dick, yes, if we expect to be effective.
Now granted, that makes things a bit fuzzy at times.

DICK: For the public?

NORM: For people. Yes. That's right.

DICK: To take it all in, all the ins and outs.
The ups and downs from day to day.
Or just to keep track of all the players involved.
The names—

NORM: Yes, a lot of them are hard to pronounce.

DICK: Not to mention all the different departments and agencies.
All those acronyms. Letters. Numbers.

NORM: It's too much for any one mind to track.

DICK: Clearly.

NORM: The point is not to become preoccupied.

DICK: With every little twist and turn.

NORM: Exactly. You can drive yourself crazy that way.

DICK: Trying to actually understand what's happening.

NORM: It's unknown territory we're into here, Dick.

DICK: Unknowable territory?

NORM: Hard to say.

DICK: In any event, the old rules don't apply?

NORM: Some of them, Dick. Some still do.

DICK: And others don't.

NORM: No. That's right.
Or they do, at the moment—

DICK: And then later they don't.

NORM: Right, and then later—

DICK: They do again?

NORM: Not really. No. But sometimes they do.
And sometimes, we need to say they do.

DICK: Even though they don't.

NORM: In reality, no.

DICK:
You address this in the book. This shifting reality.

NORM: It's more our perspective than reality, really.

DICK: How we view this war. Against extremism.
Or terror. Or whatever we're calling it now.

NORM: It doesn't really matter what we call it, Dick.
They're just words, names, which refer to the thing—

DICK: The thing we mean...whatever we call it.
The facts. The reality. That the words refer to.

NORM: Yes, that's critically important, Dick.
We need to keep our eye on the ball here
and not get distracted by what it all means.

DICK: But, whatever it is, it is a *war*.
A war on *something*.

NORM: Right. Sure.

DICK: Call it what you want, the facts don't change.

NORM: No. Of course not.

DICK: That's the reality.

NORM: Right. Look, what we've got here, Dick,
regardless of what words or labels we use,
and what they do or do not mean,
is a fundamental clash of values.

DICK: An irreconcilable clash of values?

NORM: Compromise is out of the question.

DICK: So no room for diplomacy or negotiation.

NORM:
I'm afraid not, Dick. There's just no common ground.
It's us or them.

DICK: The extremists.

NORM: Yes.

DICK: The final threat.

NORM: There is no other threat.

DICK: None?

NORM: O K, there are threats. Sure.
There are always threats. But nothing on the scale—

DICK: Manageable threats. Nothing we can't handle.

NORM: Nothing that rises to this level, no.
Look, we're in a different situation now—

DICK: It's a new world, isn't it?

NORM: Absolutely.
The world we knew, of major conflicts,
World War One, Two, Three—

DICK: The Cold War.

NORM: Right, and all the others,
the whole idea of wars between nations,
the concept of nations and peoples itself,
extending back five thousand years—

DICK: Five thousand years?

NORM: To Ancient Sumer.

DICK: So the entire history of western civilization.

NORM: Pretty much. Yeah. That world is gone.

DICK: Gone?

NORM: Gone.

DICK: Over.

NORM: Done.
We're talking total paradigm shift here.

DICK: The end of history?

NORM: Well, I don't know about that.
Look, I don't want to get too academic
and bore your viewers completely to death.
Let's just say it's a whole new ballgame,
which calls for a whole new set of assumptions.

DICK: So we need to adjust people's expectations.

NORM: It's one of the main reasons I wrote the book.

DICK: To help people adjust the way they see things.

NORM: It's absolutely paramount, Dick.
Folks need to know what they're up against.

DICK: And not just in terms of a terrorist attack,
but the psychological aspects as well?

NORM: We need folks to be able to protect themselves,
and their families, of course, in these uncertain times.

DICK: And you believe the public is prepared to
    accept—

NORM: I do, Dick. I believe that strongly.
I'm absolutely convinced of that fact.
We have to start treating the public like adults.
Level with people. Tell them the truth.

DICK: The truth.

NORM: Right. Within limits, of course.

DICK: Knowing that some secrets will need to remain—

NORM: Secret. Sure. Look, we all want transparency,
full disclosure, accountability—

DICK: Just not at the expense of security concerns.

NORM: Right. No. And people get that.
They're not children. They understand.
The American public doesn't need to know,
or necessarily even *want* to know,
every little detail of what we're doing.
Who is being detained where
on suspicion of what, on the orders of whom.

DICK: But people do want to be told what's happening.

NORM: Of course. Yes. In a general way.

DICK: Just not the details.

NORM: Exactly, no.
Listen, the last thing we want to do
is confuse the public even more than it is.

DICK: O K—

NORM: And, Dick, I can assure your viewers,
that every resource we have at our disposal
is being brought directly to bear.

DICK: Good to hear. So there are hopeful signs.

NORM: Well...I wouldn't want to go that far.

DICK: No?

NORM: No. I mean, we're not out of the woods here.

DICK: We're not?

NORM: No. Not by a long shot.

DICK: O K. So...where does that leave us?

NORM: Pardon?

DICK: You just said, we're not out of the woods.

NORM: Right. I just said that.

DICK: Right. So...
if we're not out of the woods, where *are* we then?

NORM: Well, obviously, we're still *in* the woods, Dick.

DICK: O K, but—

NORM: I mean, you're either somewhere or you're not.

DICK: Of course.

NORM: See, Dick, there are certain stages,
certain clearly definable stages
that every crisis passes through.

DICK: O K—

NORM:
And at the moment, we're between two of those stages.

DICK: Between two stages.

NORM: That's where we are.

DICK: So in a state of readiness...anticipation.

NORM: I think that's an accurate representation.

DICK: Of where we are.

NORM: At the moment, yes.

DICK:
Alright. Good. Now, I want to flesh this out some.
I'd like to talk about extremism itself.
Now, as you pointed out so well in your book,
we use the word. We say it every day.
What are we actually talking about?

NORM: Well Dick, that's tough. It's difficult to define.
In an abstract sense, rather than with examples.
I mean, we all recognize it when we see it, don't we?
But a textbook definition—

DICK: Violence?

NORM: Yes.
Violence is key. A key component.

DICK: A defining component?

NORM: I'd say so, yes.

DICK: The use of violence for political aims.

NORM: Or advocating the use of violence.
I mean, I think the Webster's definition is
acts or whatever that are beyond the pale.

DICK: Outside the norm.

NORM: Of what's accepted.

DICK: Acceptable means of reform or redress.

NORM: Which civilized people deem appropriate.

DICK: The overwhelming majority of people.

NORM: Sure. I mean, take your viewers, for example,
the people who are watching this show right now.
They know an extremist act when they see one.
You don't need a PhD or anything.

DICK: It's common sense. Self-evident.

NORM: Right.

DICK: And that's true regardless of one's political
  leanings.

NORM: Makes absolutely no difference at all.

DICK: Whether you come at it from the left or the right.

NORM: No.

DICK: Or whatever political perspective.
I mean, your organization, the CASS,
is considered by many, to be, well,
rather conservative, is it not?

NORM: We think of ourselves as centrist, actually.

DICK: But more center right, then left, right?

NORM: It really depends on the issue, Dick.
We try to take a pragmatic approach.

DICK: Common sense, as opposed to ideology.

NORM: Frankly, Dick, I think these distinctions
are somewhat less than helpful at this point.

DICK: Really?

NORM: Yes, I think we've moved beyond them.

DICK: Beyond the traditional ideological labels?

NORM: Except in the most superficial sense.

DICK: I guess they don't really mean much, do they?
Beyond the horse race. The competition.

NORM: Now, that's not to say there's no daylight at all.

DICK: Between the parties?

NORM: Right. I mean,
there *are* still those issues where we *do* disagree.
I wouldn't want your viewers to get the wrong
  impression.

It's essential that we still maintain the two parties.
The two points of view. You know what I mean.

DICK: Conservative and Liberal.

NORM: Left and Right.

DICK: So folks can identify, with one or the other,
and root for their party.

NORM: Absolutely.
I mean, it wouldn't be much of a democracy, would it,
if there were just one party, with no opposition?

DICK: True.

NORM: Or, you know, if there were still the two
   parties,
but the difference between them was virtually
   cosmetic—

DICK: Because they all represented the same big
interests.

NORM: Right. Rather than the people themselves.

DICK: Like they do. In reality.

NORM: In America. Right.

DICK: Thank God.

NORM: Yes, thank God, Dick.

DICK: So American democracy is alive and well then?

NORM: No question, Dick. No doubt about it.
No, America may have its problems.
But it's still the most powerful democracy on earth.

DICK: Regardless of whatever minor disagreements
or differences of opinion between the two parties.

NORM:
No, on the contrary, it's precisely those differences
that keep our democracy flourishing, Dick.
I mean, look at the Senate. Look at the House.

There's real democratic debate going on.
O K, so they all play golf together
and they all raise money from the same corporations.
But that doesn't mean there isn't real opposition—

DICK: On social policy. Abortion. Race.
Immigration. That kind of thing.

NORM: Yes. It's just that all those other issues,
important though they are, pale in comparison
and become irrelevant—

DICK: In comparison to the threat.

NORM: Exactly, Dick. And rightfully so.
I mean, that's the beauty and strength of our
    democracy.
We can fight all day over the little things,
healthcare, education and all,
but, you know, when the chips are really down,
we come together, to face, well,
whatever it is we happen to be facing.

DICK: And that's true of any democracy, isn't it?

NORM: Yes, it is. It's a hallmark, actually.
You see it throughout history. Rome, for example.
And you see it now. Around this issue.
Throughout the world. There's no real dissent.
The world is united. It's marching in lockstep.
It's quite historic, when you think about it.
All of the major democracies in the world
working together, like one big machine,
to face this enemy—

DICK: Extremism.

NORM: Yes.

DICK:
It's in all of our interests, is the point you're making.
What with global markets and communications—

NORM: Yes, it's one big global network now.
One seamless system. There's no escape.
It's finally, truly, the Age of Democracy.

DICK: That's quite a statement.

NORM: We are on the brink.
All the dominoes are falling our way.

DICK: Except for the extremists.

NORM: Except for the extremists.

DICK: This is what you mean by the "final threat."
The final threat to a democratic world,
united, at last, under a single system,
with no remaining outside opposition.

NORM: That's the vision. That's the dream.

DICK: Democracy reigning unopposed.

NORM: Throughout the world. For a thousand years.
It's so close, Dick. I don't think people realize
how close we are to achieving that dream.

DICK: This is the focus of the first half of your book.
This moment of danger on the brink of victory.
This last desperate gasp of resistance,
which has no chance of succeeding, you propose.

NORM: No, not in the long run. No.
The writing is on the wall, Dick.

DICK: It's destiny then.

NORM: Destiny. Right.
Democracy is destiny. Always was.
Always will be.

DICK: Beautiful vision.

NORM: To us, yes. To freedom-loving people.

DICK: But not to the extremists?

NORM: No. On the contrary.
They're terrified of it.

DICK: Of democracy?

NORM: Yes.
These folks are not blind. They see what's coming.
They know it signals the end for them.

DICK: Their power, values—

NORM: Their whole way of life.

DICK: Fundamentalism?

NORM: Radicalism.
Opposition. In all its forms.

DICK: But not dissent, or peaceful protest.

NORM: No, of course not. Dissent is fine.
People can protest till they're blue in the face,
blow off steam, get it out of their systems,
express their opinions—

DICK: But that's different, right?
Because it poses no threat.

NORM: No, it's completely harmless.

DICK: It has absolutely no potential
to threaten the system or change anything.

NORM: No. Just the opposite, in fact.
Symbolic protest, self-expression,
walking around all day with signs,
chanting slogans...that empowers people.

DICK: And it's pretty good cardiovascular exercise.

NORM: Sure, marching, working those puppets—

DICK: Aren't those great, those giant puppets?

NORM: Some of those protesters are real artists.

DICK: But again, they pose no tangible threat.

NORM: No. Those things are like concerts, Dick.
They set up stages. There are speeches, music.
Folks make a day of it, bring the kids.
You march around town for a couple hours,
go home, look for yourself on the news.
Come Monday morning, it's back to work.

DICK: Which, I guess, brings us back to violence then,
back to the willingness to use violence.

NORM: That's what's really at the core of it, Dick.
That is what's absolutely unacceptable.

DICK: The whole idea of using violence,
sabotage, these guerilla tactics.

NORM: Or even just putting the question out there.

DICK: I'm not sure I follow.

NORM: See, that's how it starts.
They put these questions out there, you know,
as if they merited consideration.

DICK: Rather than there being a foregone conclusion.

NORM: It conflates the two opposing sides.

DICK: As if there were actually something to discuss.

NORM: Right.

DICK: Which there isn't.

NORM: No, of course not.
Their goal is not to *answer* the question.
Their goal is to get the question out there.

DICK: Out there into people's minds,
to get them thinking.

NORM: To *frame* their thinking.

DICK: According to the terms of the question posed.

NORM: Sure, because once you admit the question,
once you allow it to enter your mind,
see, they've got you.

DICK: The extremists.

NORM: Yes.
They've sucked you into their twisted logic.

DICK: They have?

NORM: Sure.

DICK: Because you're asking their question?

NORM:
You're doubting yourself. You're getting confused.

DICK: You're thinking too much.

NORM: You're over-thinking.
You're complicating something essentially simple.

DICK: For example?

NORM: Well, O K, for example,
you might start looking back at history and, you know,
asking yourself, "What government, or system,
was ever fundamentally changed
by anything *other* than violence, ever?"

DICK: Wow. That *is* a dangerous question.

NORM:
That's why we don't even want to formulate it, Dick.
We don't even want to put it into words.

DICK: Because we'd just be playing into their hands,
   you mean,
opening up a Pandora's Box?

NORM: We'd be opening up a whole can of worms.

DICK: Letting the genie out of the bottle.

NORM: That's right, Dick. And as we all know,
once you let that genie out,
you're never going to get it back in there, are you?

DICK: No.

NORM: No. And then they've got you.
You're lost in their game. Your head starts going.

DICK:
You start thinking all these complicated thoughts,
asking questions that lead you nowhere.

NORM: Right, they just lead you around in circles,
round and round, round and round,
until your head is so full of all these ideas
you can't tell your ass from a hole in the ground.

DICK: So the goal is, don't let the genie out.
Never open that can of worms.

NORM: Keep things simple. Stick to the facts.

DICK: O K. Good. So...what are the facts?

NORM:
The facts are the facts, Dick. They're black and white.

DICK: Black and white.

NORM: In this case, yes.
I mean, we like to say things are never black and white,
but they kind of are, aren't they, in the end?

DICK: Are they?

NORM: Sure. Look at the world.
What do you got? You got this conflict.
You got democracy, in whatever form it takes,
versus extremism. This is where we are.

DICK: This is the world?

NORM: This is it.

DICK: This is the conflict. The final conflict.

NORM: Cut and dried. Black and white.

DICK: A story. A conflict...between good and evil.

NORM: Or at least between two opposing sides.

DICK: A war. What could be simpler than that?

NORM: Nothing. But see, the problem is,
it's war, sure, but like the war on crime,
or the war on drugs, or the war on whatever.

DICK: The war on poverty. The war on cancer.

NORM: We're not going eradicate *crime*, are we?
Poverty? Anti-social behavior?

DICK: No.

NORM: There will always be criminals, won't there?
The point is to control and manage it, right?

DICK: But we're talking about the entire world.

NORM: Exactly, Dick. The entire world.
The world community. The global market.

DICK: Like the United States of the Entire World.

NORM: Something like that. Sure, right.

DICK: But aren't we jumping the gun here, Norm?
I mean, the world is not united *yet*.

NORM: Isn't it, Dick? Take a good look.
Take a hard look, and tell me what you see.
You don't see countries fighting countries anymore.
Do you? O K, little bitty countries, sure,
that we can walk into any time we want.
But not *real* countries. I mean, try to imagine.
Are we going to go to war with China?

DICK: No.

NORM: No, of course we're not.
Democracies don't fight democracies, do they?

DICK: Well, China's not really a democracy, is it?

NORM: They're a market economy.

DICK: That's different.

NORM: O K.
Democracy. Republic. Market economy.
I think you know what I'm saying, Dick.
And I think your viewers understand what I mean.
You've got the civilized world, the democratic world,
the community of nations, of civilized nations,
free market economies, or whatever you want to call
      them,
the countries that are playing *ball*, basically,
whatever internal problems they may have,
and then, what you've got, is not really an enemy,
not really an enemy country or anything,
or even a coherent or consistent ideology,
but rather, this epidemic of extremism,
both within and without these countries, Dick.

DICK: An epidemic. Like a virus or something.

NORM: Yes. Like a virus. Or a cancer in the body.

DICK: In the global body.

NORM: In the organs. Right.
O K, and maybe there's more in one organ than
      another.
Still, all the organs depend on each other.
The Middle East is the prostate, say.
Southeast Asia could be the pancreas.

DICK:
Western Europe would be the lungs or something.

NORM: Sure. Whatever. You get the idea.
The point is, Dick, we got prostate cancer.
And now it's spreading all over the body,
metastasizing into the other organs.

DICK: Into the pancreas.

NORM: Into the brain.
We have to get that cancer, Dick.
We have to cure it, wipe it out.
Here. The cancer is here, inside.
It's in here with us, hiding, among us.
Think for a minute. Ask yourself,
who, exactly, is the enemy here?

DICK: Is it not the extremists?

NORM: Of course. Of course.
But who, exactly, *are* these extremists?

DICK: I thought...al Qaeda, Islamic Jihad—

NORM:
They're just *names*, Dick. They're just words. Labels.
Hezbollah. Al Qaeda. Whatever.
Militias. Factions. ETA. The FARC.
The R A F. The R T S.

DICK:
The names and faces change, is what you're saying.

NORM: Exactly. See, we're not fighting a regime,
or a country, or even these groups, really.
No. It's a way of looking at the world.

DICK: A way of viewing—

NORM: The world.

DICK: Reality.

NORM: That's what we need to address and correct.

DICK:
So we need to correct how these people see the world.
Regardless of their particular fanatical beliefs.

NORM: They all have one thing in common, Dick.
A common enemy.

DICK: America?

NORM: No.
Democracy, Dick. Freedom itself.

DICK: This is why they bomb things inside their own
    countries.

NORM: It's not just other countries, Dick.
The cancer has spread. It's everywhere now.
Here. England. Spain. You name it.
All over the world. No one's immune.
We can't just keep blasting away at the symptoms.
We need to get this cancer at the roots.

DICK: So we need to address this way of seeing.
This extremist way of seeing the world.

NORM: Yes, but first and foremost, Dick,
we need to stop them spreading their views.
That's the virus. That's the danger.

DICK:
That more and more people will follow their beliefs?

NORM: Not just beliefs, Dick. It's deeper than that.
There are all kinds of fringe beliefs out there.

DICK: So you're saying, it's more about where they are
on the spectrum than what they actually believe.

NORM: Extremism is extremism, Dick.
Once you're out there on the fringe, you're out there.
Islamic terrorists. Eco-terrorists.
Christian militias. Unrepentant Communists.
These people who blow up S U Vs.

DICK: The Unabomber.

NORM: Radicals, Dick.
Radicalism, in all its forms.
Look, you can rattle off a thousand examples.
What particular brand of extremist nonsense
they happen to believe in is beside the point.
What's important is, they've crossed the line.

DICK: They're spreading extremist propaganda.

NORM: Oh, we're way beyond propaganda here, Dick.
We're talking about programming people's minds.

DICK: Brainwashing suicide bombers and so on.

NORM: Sure, but that's just the most extreme example.
Suicide bombers. Manchurian candidates.
I'm afraid the reality is much more subtle.
Insidiously and surreptitiously subtle.
Look, I want to try to make this concrete.
Let's just use us as an example, O K?

DICK: Us?

NORM: Us. You and me.
And your viewers, watching this show, right now.
Now, you and I are standing here talking.
On television, right? Talking about freedom.
And we know what we mean, don't we?
You and I? Your viewers, at home?
Or the vast majority, in any event?
We know what we mean when we use the word
    freedom.

DICK: Yes. Of course. Freedom means freedom.

NORM: To us, Dick, sure. We know that.
But they don't know that.

DICK: The extremists.

NORM: Right.

DICK: They don't know that freedom means freedom?

NORM: No. Of course not. That's the problem.
See...it isn't freedom they hate.

DICK: It isn't?

NORM: No. Of course not, Dick.
No one hates freedom.

DICK: It's impossible, right?

NORM: Right. Yes. But see, to them,
freedom isn't freedom. They hear the word,
but to them it means something else entirely.

DICK: What?

NORM: Something we can't even imagine.

DICK: Because we're not them.

NORM: No. Right.

DICK: But something bad, in any event.

NORM: No question, Dick. Something threatening.
Some huge unstoppable historical force
coming to wipe them off the face of the earth
and strip them of the very last remnants of their values.

DICK: Their religious values...cultural values.

NORM: It's a horrible thing to contemplate, Dick,
the annihilation of a people's values.
I mean, some people have had them for hundreds of
   years.

DICK: They just take them for granted. For the way
   things are.

NORM: Exactly. Yes. We do it too.
Everyone does. It's human nature.

DICK: You have to believe what you believe is real.
Or else you'd just go insane, wouldn't you?

NORM: Sure. Again, take us, for example.
Take this show. Politics in Focus.

DICK: Issues in Focus.

NORM: Issues. Whatever.
The show we're doing. What we're actually doing.
Now, *we* all know what it is, right?
Us. Your viewers. We know how it works.
We've seen these shows a thousand times.
We've seen them since the time we were kids.

We know how they work. There's nothing to question.
You're the anchor. I'm the expert.
I wrote some book. We're talking about it.
The target audience is a small minority
of affluent, educated urban professionals.

DICK: People who read and maybe go to museums.

NORM: Sure, museums, galleries, theater.
And see, we just take all that for granted.
We recognize it automatically.
We don't have to ask ourselves what it *is*,
what it's trying to *do* or anything.

DICK: What it is is a given, is what you're saying.

NORM: Yes. But now take some *extremist*, Dick,
watching this show from their perspective.
Imagine for a moment, that one of your viewers,
someone watching this show, right now,
listening to what I'm saying right now,
were one of them.

DICK: An extremist.

NORM: Yes.
See, to *them*, this wouldn't be what it is,
the show that it is, that we know it to be.

DICK: What would it be? Some kind of propaganda?
Part of some complex capitalist conspiracy?

NORM: Sure. It would seem like something staged.

DICK: Fake.

NORM: Not fake, but a simulation.

DICK: Staged to look like a real conversation.

NORM: The usual meaningless beltway blather.

DICK: Something that would just be on in the house
while you were making dinner or whatever you were
   doing.

NORM: Seeping into your unconscious mind.
Reinforcing your psychic programming.

DICK: Or, I suppose, if you were one of them,
subtly undermining your entire world view,
eating away at your core beliefs.

NORM: More than just your beliefs, Dick.
Actually altering the way you perceive.
Programming your perception itself.
This is the battle...the *real* battle.

DICK: The battle for hearts and minds, you mean.

NORM: It's so much more than just hearts and minds.
It's about how people perceive *reality*.
Look, as long as people are allowed to believe,
to see the world through that extremist lens,
no amount of soldiers is ever going to be enough.
We're never going to beat this threat that way.

DICK: So it's people's minds that need to change.

NORM: People's perceptions. Precisely, Dick.

DICK:
How people interpret what they're seeing and hearing.

NORM: And how we perceive the problem itself.
We've been looking at it through the same old lens.
The same expectations. All these old assumptions—

DICK:
About how to interpret what's happening in the world.

NORM: Right in front of our faces, Dick.
We're looking right at it, and we can't even see it.
We cannot see what is actually happening.
Right now. Right in front of our faces.

DICK: Because all we know is what we knew.
We're blinded by what we expect to see.
What we've always seen. What we've been trained to
  see.

NORM: All we know is, whatever it is,
that is actually happening, in front of our faces,
isn't what is supposed to be happening.

DICK: And what *is* it that is actually happening?

NORM: There you go, Dick. That's it right there.
People want answers. They're asking these questions.
They're looking. Listening. They want to understand.
But if the world they're looking at no longer reflects
   them?

DICK: What *does* it reflect?

NORM: Exactly. Nothing.

DICK: Nothing familiar.

NORM: It's rather disturbing.
An unsettling picture, in truth, Dick.
And, of course, that's precisely the effect they want.

DICK: The extremists.

NORM: Right. Uncertainty. Doubt.
Pessimism. Cynicism. Fatalism. Fear.

DICK:
Are you saying that people are wrong to be afraid?

NORM: Now, I don't think anyone is saying that.
The threat is there. It's not going away.
But that doesn't mean life can't go on as normal.

DICK: It has to, doesn't it?

NORM: Yes. It does.
No matter what happens. Or doesn't happen.
Look, some of this is purely theoretical.

DICK: Hypothetical.

NORM: Yeah. You bet.
I mean, for all we know, there could be someone right
   now,
in Washington, or London, with a nuclear bomb.

DICK: Or putting Anthrax in the subway in New York.

NORM: Those fears are real. Those are possibilities.

DICK: Eventualities, some would say.

NORM: Sure. But we have to behave as if they're not, keeping in mind, of course, that they are.

DICK: Eventualities?

NORM: Hypothetically.

DICK: Theoretically.

NORM: Absolutely.
Look, any way you slice it, Dick,
the world is divided. It's badly divided.
It's dangerously divided, Dick.

DICK: And we're trying to put it back together?

NORM:
Or at least some semblance. That's what folks want.

DICK: A cohesive picture of a coherent world.

NORM:
Something that people can look at and recognize.

DICK: And understand.

NORM: And take for granted.

DICK: So...restore stability. Basic order.

NORM: Order, yes, that's it exactly.
It's this perception of chaos that's causing anxiety.

DICK: The *perception* of chaos.

NORM: It's corrosive, Dick.
It erodes trust. It divides people.
People feel it. Of course they feel it.
I guarantee you, they're feeling it right now.

DICK: The divide. The rift.

NORM: It's like a gaping wound.
Like a big gaping wound that will not heal.

DICK: Like a hole torn in the fabric of the real.

NORM:
Yes, and we need to fill that hole with something.

DICK: Fill in the blanks. Restore the plot.

NORM: Make it clear who the characters are.
Who's the protagonist. Who's the antagonist.
Basic Aristotelean poetics.

DICK: So we're talking about finding some new frame
   of reference—

NORM: We have to, Dick. This doesn't work.

DICK: This feeling of formlessness and ambiguity.
This sense that nothing really *means* anything,
or leads us anywhere, or clarifies anything.

NORM: People want something concrete to believe in.
They need it. People always have.
They're reaching for it now, but there's nothing there,
nothing but this empty shapeless void—

DICK: Where something solid and real used to be.

NORM: Or the appearance of something solid and real.

DICK: In which we're no longer able to believe.

NORM: Right. You know what it's like, Dick?
It's like after the first affair in a marriage.
Or the birth of photography...what it did to painting.
I mean, sure, you can still get your portrait painted.
You're still married—

DICK: But it's not the same.

NORM: No. It isn't. It's completely different.

DICK: Because you can't go back—

NORM: No, you can't.
You have to go forward. We, as a nation,
have to go forward. There's just too much at stake.
We have to be proactive here.
The word action. It needs repeating.
We have to take *action* on the situation.

DICK: On the situation as it exists.

NORM: We can't just sit by like *spectators*, Dick,
and let things happen that are out of our control.

DICK: Sit there passively and watch things evolve.

NORM: We need to learn how to steer this thing, Dick.
I mean, *somebody* is going to end up steering it.
If not us, then somebody else.

DICK: To steer...what?

NORM: This. Now.
The world. Look, the old world is gone.
It's over. It's gone. It is not there.
Look around. Do you see it anywhere?

DICK: No.

NORM: No. Because it isn't there.
But we're still operating as if it were there.

DICK: So... what *is* there, looks and sounds—

NORM: Incomprehensible. Like utter nonsense.

DICK: How could we say anything meaningful about it
when we don't even know what it *is* yet?

NORM:
It's like looking into one of those fun-house mirrors.

DICK: Or a broken mirror...like a Picasso painting.

NORM: Except that it's even worse than that, Dick.
With Picasso things were still what they were,
all broken up, but you could fit them together,
whereas now what you have is this shape-shifting

    mess,
where everything seems to be consuming itself.

DICK: Like that snake that's always eating its own tail.

NORM: The Ouroboros, yes, or Quetzalcoatl.

DICK: Or like one of those little Russian dolls
that you open and there's all those other dolls.

NORM: It's half-truths hiding inside of lies
all wrapped up in spin and peppered with jargon.

DICK: Which, on the surface, sounds kind of normal.
More or less like what you're used to hearing.

NORM: It's all aimed at your unconscious mind.

DICK: Like some kind of neuro-linguistic programming.

NORM: Burrowing into your unconscious brain,
physically changing the way you perceive,
the way you hear things, how you think.

DICK:
You're trying to keep up, but your head is spinning.

NORM: You're running in circles, inside a wheel.

DICK: Like one of those little hamster wheels
where the hamster keeps running and running and
    running—

NORM: Until all you want is to get off the wheel,
get back to normal, where things make sense.

DICK: Or seem to make sense.

NORM: Or at least sound familiar.

DICK: The words at least, within the context.

NORM: People saying recognizable things.

DICK: Even if you have no idea what they mean.

NORM:
Buzzwords. Euphemisms. Government-Speak.

DICK: Things that seem to have the ring of truth.

NORM: See, problem is, Dick, we eat that stuff up.

DICK: Us. Everyone.

NORM: People. Right.
The American people. People with *jobs*.
And *kids* in college. *Taxpayers*, Dick.
They're the ones bearing the brunt of this thing.
They're the ones getting the short end of the stick.
Now, these people have been betrayed and lied to
   enough.
It's been going on for years and years.
It's gotten to the point where it's what they expect.

DICK:
Being given the run-around, lied to, manipulated?

NORM:
Precisely. And we need to change that perception.

DICK: This cynicism. This disbelief.

NORM:
We need folks to be able to believe they can trust us.

DICK: Trust the government and the media and so on.

NORM: The folks in charge.

DICK: Authorities.

NORM: Right.
Or at least to trust that we know what we're doing.
That we have a plan. That we're in control.

Dick   Even if everything seems like chaos.

Norm   Right. Yes.

DICK: Which it isn't.

NORM: No.

DICK: But even if it were, we'd deny it, wouldn't we?

NORM: Yes, we'd be forced to.

DICK: But it's not, is what we're saying.
That it's *not* the reality. That's what we're saying.

NORM: Right. No. Not yet, anyway.

DICK: O K, so...what *is* the reality?

NORM: Exactly, Dick. That's the question.

DICK: I meant specifically. In terms of policy.

NORM: Look, Dick. We're fighting a *war* here.
Another world war. Let's call it what it is.
It's World War Four. It's for all the marbles.
Policy is going to shift and change.
That doesn't mean anything. Not in itself.
What we need to bear in mind is the threat.
The constantly changing nature of the threat.
The extremist threat. The terrorist threat.
The repetition of the word threat.

DICK: And pictures of threatening-looking people?

NORM: Sure, you know, as long as they're plausible.
But look, we can't afford to get reckless.
We can't just ram *anything* down the public's throat.
Not without the appearance of broad support.

DICK: Which we have, do we not?

NORM: Sure, if we need it.
But even if we don't, it doesn't really matter.
Still, it's essential that we make the effort,
or at least be seen to be making the effort.

DICK: Internationally, you mean.

NORM: No, here, at home.
We want to keep the focus here.
At least for the moment. Later we can change it.

DICK: But for now, at least, for the time being—

NORM: Yes. We need to stay the course,
regardless of what direction we take
or consider taking at a later time.

DICK: Which may never actually arrive.

NORM:
Exactly. I mean, we won't know till we get there.

DICK: Or don't get there.

NORM: Look, the point is, Dick,
the American people are demanding our attention
here at home, which is understandable,
especially now, what with everything else
going on elsewhere all over the world,
which also demands our full attention,
which the American people, of course, support—

DICK: So are we seeing what amounts to a growing
     weariness,
an exhaustion of compassion for these foreign
     interventions?

NORM: Now, I would challenge anyone challenging the
     compassion
of the American people, as a people, Dick,
particularly when it comes to intervention.

DICK: Even if it means more troops in harms way?

NORM: Now, hold on, Dick. Hold on right there.
I think both parties have made it crystal clear
that they are strongly against seeing our young men
     and women
sacrificed needlessly, or for dubious reasons,
unless the situation absolutely warrants.

DICK: And does it?

NORM: Of course. We think it does.
We believe it does. Everyone does.
But this is America, which means, ultimately,

it's up to the American people to decide.
Now, we remain confident in the American people,
in their goodness, and strength, and their ability to
    choose
good over evil, when the choice is clear.
Look, just because we've entered some post-everything
    age,
where everything is relative and essentially
    meaningless,
that doesn't mean people can't tell right from wrong,
or the truth from a lie.

DICK: What's real and what's fake.

NORM: The American people are not stupid, Dick.
People can tell when they're being played with.
This isn't Nazi Germany here.
You can't just feed the American people
some made-up facts, show them some pictures,
tap into their latent racist paranoia,
and go off and invade some other country.

DICK: No. Of course—

NORM: And I'll tell you something else.
One thing our polling *consistently* confirms,
is that the public is fed up with all these games,
with politicians and pundits and experts
running this nation's affairs like, you know,
one of those Hollywood monster movies,
where the monster keeps jumping out all the time,
every thirty or forty-five seconds,
punching your buttons, tapping your fear,
working your emotions like the strings on a puppet.
People just won't put up with it anymore.

DICK: No?

NORM: No. It's not like the old days.
People want to hear the truth.
The simple truth.

DICK: Is there such a thing?

NORM: No. Of course not. Don't be ridiculous.

DICK: It's all so hopelessly complicated, isn't it?

NORM: Yes, the truth is, it's unimaginable.
Our brains would explode if we ever got a glimpse.

DICK: It would be like trying to do quantum physics
on L S D in Chinese or something.

NORM: That's why they want us to *make* it simple.

DICK: Which we're trying to do.

NORM: Exactly. Right.
Simple. Clear. This is what sells.
Not all this multiplicitous nonsense.
If this is what people wanted, well—

DICK: They certainly wouldn't be watching us.

NORM: No. Not at all. They'd be off reading poetry
or watching some French film by Jean Luc Godard.

DICK: Where you have to concentrate every second,
analyze everything you see and hear,
constantly aware of your own perception
perceiving itself perceiving itself.

NORM: And who wants to live like that, right?

DICK: No one.

NORM: No. What you want...is
to be able to relax, and forget, and enjoy.

DICK: And not be reminded of what's actually
happening.

NORM: The machine at work.

DICK: At work on your mind.

NORM: Flipping little switches.

DICK: Turning things on.

NORM: Punching buttons.

DICK: Testing. Probing.

NORM: Patching new wires into old connections,
firing up circuits you thought were dead.

DICK: Or ones you didn't even know you had.

NORM: Till your brain is swimming with associations,
connotations, intuitions—

DICK: You *understand*, but if someone asked you
what it *is* that you understand—

NORM: How could you possibly begin to describe it?

DICK: It's like you've been lost and in a trance,
have been for God knows how many years.

NORM:
You weren't really *there*. You *thought* you were there,
present, listening, but all you were doing
was floating along, being ferried along,
on a stream of sounds or words or phrases
that sounded like what you were used to hearing.

DICK: It's like there's this set of things that people say,
and it sort of meshes in there without you noticing.

NORM: It washes over you, wave after wave.
Wave after wave. It just keeps coming.

DICK: And what, you just surrender to it eventually?

NORM: It's nearly impossible not to, Dick.
Thing is, there's so much happening so fast now,
new information coming at you all the time,
that you have to focus on every other minute.
Wars. Scandals. Terrorist attacks.

DICK: Software updates. Things that give you cancer.

NORM: Most of the time it's all you can do
just to process the new information you're fed.

DICK: You're surrounded by screens of talking heads.

NORM: Phones ringing. Computers beeping.
T Vs blaring at you everywhere you go.

DICK: It's like a symphony of random noise.

NORM: Drowning out your inner thoughts.

DICK: You're fighting so hard to follow something
whose entire purpose is to get you lost.

NORM: It's exhausting is what it is, Dick.
It numbs the mind. Physically. It does.
It just beats the life right out of you, really,
until you're just this empty husk of a person,
all medicated up and numb inside.
But, hey, that comes with the territory, right?
That's part and parcel of a free society.

DICK: You have to take the good with the bad.

NORM: Sure. I mean, what's the alternative?
Communism?! Socialism?! Fundamentalism?
Hey, no problem with confusion *there*!
No problem with orientation *there*!
No Sir, *there* you know exactly where you are,
each and every second, don't you, Dick?

DICK:
I suppose that's true. Because it's all been dictated—

NORM: You bet it's dictated. It's handed down.
Down from on high.

DICK: By dictators.

NORM: Sure.
Look, you can go at this a thousand ways.
At the end of the day, the choice is the same.
You either want *freedom*, to do and say the *truth*,
or you want to live in some country where you can't
  even *own* things
and the government wants to control what you *think*,
to control *the way* you think even.

DICK:
How they've *trained* you to think since early childhood.

NORM:
Where they keep you lost and ignorant and confused
and feeling completely powerless and alone...
You sit there staring at the television,
at the same re-packaged propaganda,
for thirty or forty or fifty years,
until you can't even carry on a conversation.

DICK: You get together with your family or friends
and all you can do is talk about products.

NORM: Right! And then, on a show like this, say,
you couldn't just come out here and talk straight with
    people.
Not like we're doing. No. Oh no!
If you wanted to say anything that actually *mattered*,
or had the potential to *change* anything,
you couldn't just come out here and say it openly.

DICK: No?

NORM: No. You'd have to *sneak* it in there.

DICK: Sneak it in there in *code*, you mean,
like they used to do in Russia, or Czechoslovakia,
to fool the censors—

NORM: Right. But see,
it's even trickier than that now, Dick.
I mean, let's say you do manage to sneak yourself in
    there,
sneak your little Trojan horse in there,
right there, inside the enemy camp,
and start sending out your subversive little *code*—

DICK:
You mean, what if the enemy had broken your code?

NORM: Or even worse, Dick, imagine for a moment...
What if the enemy didn't *have to* break your code,

because they're the ones that *generated* the code *for* you,
in some horribly evil and insidious way
that allowed you to think that *you* had invented it?
Here you think you're being really clever
but in reality the whole thing is one big *set-up*
sucking you into where they wanted you in the first
　place,
into a position where you're completely *harmless*
and they don't even have to decode your messages
or bother keeping an eye on you at all
because you're only saying what they *allowed* you to
　say,
what they *trained* you to say, how they *trained* you to
　say it.

DICK: O K. So...what are we talking about?
Are we talking censorship? Self-censorship? What?

NORM: Something like that. Again, Dick,
you have to try to see all this through their eyes.
Just imagine for a minute, that you were the enemy.
One of the enemy.

DICK:　　　　　　　　An extremist.

NORM:　　　　　　　　　　　　Yes.
It's almost impossible to imagine, I know.

DICK:
And everything looked upside down and backwards,
all twisted around and paranoid, right?

NORM: Try to imagine, if you saw things that way,
how you would think, how you would see America,
and not just America, the whole Western world.
Try to imagine.

DICK:　　　　　　O K. Give me a minute.
(He tries to imagine it.)
What? You mean like... some new form of empire?

NORM: Exactly. That's the word they use.

DICK: You're joking, right?

NORM: I wish I were.

DICK: Like the Roman Empire?

NORM: For example, sure.

DICK: Like some post-industrial Pax Romana.

NORM: Not peace, exactly, but the semblance of peace.

DICK: But we don't even have the semblance of peace.

NORM: Neither did the Romans. All it meant,
the Pax Romana, was that the Empire was *there*.
Established. It was more about quashing rebellions.

DICK: Insurgent uprisings in the conquered lands.

NORM: In Carthage, the British Isles, Persia—

DICK: So, more about controlling the occupied lands,
and the conquered peoples, with their different
    cultures,
replacing their cultures with Roman culture.

NORM: Not so much replacing, Dick,
as infiltrating, reshaping, changing—

DICK: Setting up businesses, channels of trade.

NORM: Inextricably linking them to Rome.

DICK: And to Roman ways of doing things.

NORM: And looking at things. Understanding things.

DICK: Yes, O K...I'm beginning to see it.

NORM: Frightening, isn't it?

DICK: Yes, it is.
It's like they're looking at the same world we are,
the extremists, I mean—

NORM: Of course. Yes.

DICK: At the expansion of markets, culture, freedom,
everything democracy and freedom represents,

social mobility, opportunity,
freedom of expression, freedom of trade,
but seeing it, not as freedom at all,
but as some kind of system of...

NORM: Domination.

DICK: That's so insane. That's completely insane.

NORM: That's it, Dick. That's exactly the word.
It is insane. It's insanity itself.
That is exactly what we're up against.

DICK: It *is* more like we're fighting a disease,
a mental condition, than a war, isn't it?

NORM: Precisely. Yes. We're just trying to help.
We're trying to help people accept reality.

DICK: I mean, sure, there are parallels...between Rome
   and us.
But we're no empire. Not by any definition.
No sane person could make that case.
Could they?

NORM: No, Dick, we're still a Republic.

DICK: Right. Right. That's what I thought.

NORM: It's just their mental dysfunction, Dick.
Their paranoid perspective on things.
See, it's not a choice on their part.
This is how they actually perceive things.

DICK: The extremists.

NORM: Yes, I'm afraid so, Dick.

DICK: So what we all know is, in fact, *reality*,
to them, looks like—

NORM: An illusion. A lie.

DICK: Some made-up ideological system.
A fabrication. A simulation.

NORM: Pretending to be the natural world.
Common sense. The way things are.

DICK: That is so insane. Oh man.
That's completely sick.

NORM: It's sad, really.
Imagine how you'd feel. If you were one of them.
Imagine you were one of them, watching this show.

DICK: Issues in Focus?

NORM: This show. Right now.

DICK: Filtering it all through their paranoid lens.

NORM: Analyzing words, inflections, gestures.

DICK: As if this were all some elaborate performance,
carefully crafted to seem natural.

NORM: Yes, it's crazy. It's complete paranoia.
It's psychotic, Dick, is what it is.
Imagine how alone and desperate you'd feel.

DICK: Like you were living inside a simulation,
surrounded by simulations of people,
carrying on simulated conversations,
but saying nothing at all, really.

NORM: This is the way our adversary thinks.
We have to be able to understand their thinking,
how it gets inside and infiltrates everything.

DICK: *Has* it...infiltrated?

NORM: Oh, it's everywhere, Dick.
You don't always notice it right off the bat.
But it's there. Everywhere. Quietly at work.
It's there in the media. In the arts. In schools.
I mean, some of the professors we have in this country.
These de-constructionists and post-Marxist types.

DICK: In the graduate schools. The tenured radicals.

NORM: You wouldn't believe the rhetoric, Dick.
The books they've got our kids reading.
These so-called cultural theorists and scholars.
They're turning these kids into little anarchists.
They wear these masks. Attack the police.
I'm telling you, it's getting worse than the Sixties.

DICK: And in the arts as well?

NORM: Well, it's better in the arts.

DICK: Because there's no support?

NORM: Yeah, we cut all the funding.
No, the problem now is, all these tenured professors.
You can't even fire them. They can just say anything.

DICK:
But, of course, that's one of our fundamental values,
freedom of expression, freedom of speech.

NORM: Sure, of course, but within reason.
I mean, freedom of expression. Fine. Great.
But that doesn't mean you can just say whatever.

DICK: It doesn't?

NORM: No. Well, it depends where you say it.
I mean, all those artists whose funding we cut,
they're still free to express themselves,
to say what they want.

DICK: On the internet, you mean.

NORM: Sure, or in some little storefront theater.

DICK: That nobody ever goes to anyway.

NORM: There you go, Dick. It's the market at work.
Look, if normal people wanted to hear all that stuff,
all that hysterical political ranting,
and see all this perverted so-called *art*,
then these artists would be rich and famous, right?

DICK: But normal people do *not* want that.

NORM: No. Of course not. It's the last thing they want.

DICK: All this hysterical theatrics and debate.

NORM: All this pretentious political posturing.

DICK: On the part of artists. In the arts, you mean.
Or do you mean on the part of politicians?

NORM: Either. Both. It doesn't really matter.
They're all just channels of communication.
Different ways to affect people's minds.

DICK: So it's all about dissemination.

NORM: Right. It's ratings. It's market share.
It's apples and oranges. See what I mean?

DICK: Actually, I don't.

NORM: No, of course not.

DICK: I mean, are we talking about political *theater*?
Real theater...like in a *theater*?

NORM: We're talking about how these people think.

DICK: The extremists.

NORM: Yes. The terrorists, Dick.

DICK: And what does that have to do with the theater?

NORM: Nothing. Zero. That's what I meant.

DICK: One thing has nothing to do with the other.

NORM: No, of course not. Art is art.
It isn't *real*. It's, well...it's *art*.

DICK: O K. So why are we talking about it?

NORM: We're not.

DICK: We're not? We're not talking about it?

NORM: Of course not, Dick. It's just an example.
Of how their extremist thinking operates.

DICK: Oh.

NORM: See, they're like parasites, Dick.
They'll latch on to anything, and burrow in.
They'll twist the meaning of what you're saying
until it doesn't mean what it means anymore.
They'll pull at any loose thread they see
trying to get the whole thing to unravel.
O K, so I happen to be a fan of the theater,
or at least the *possibilities* of theater,
you know, people, gathered in a room,
like a congregation, those ritual roots?

DICK: You mean, where it still has some effect
on people's lives or their souls or whatever?

NORM: Right. It's true. I admit it. O K?
The point is, all that's completely irrelevant.

DICK: It is?

NORM: Sure. Look, anyone will tell you,
any politician, that there's always a degree
of theatrics, showbiz or whatever, *involved*.
You just have to keep them separate in your mind.
It's when you mix the two up that you run into
   problems.

DICK: *Political* problems. In *politics*, right?

NORM: Right. I mean, normally, who cares?
People love it. O K, fine,
maybe they don't understand the issues.
But so what, really? The *battle's* the thing.
The conflict. The action. Guys arguing over stuff.
It's good clean fun.

DICK: It's like wrestling, right?

NORM: Sure, it's just...you can take it too far.

DICK: Politics. Campaign politics, you mean.

NORM: It's pandering, Dick. It's pandering to people.
That's a tough thing to say. But sometimes, you know,

you have to call a spade a spade.
It's just plain pandering, pure and simple.
There's no other word for it. It's completely pathetic.
Look, I don't want to get us off-track with all this,
but sometimes, I just sit there and pray for a disaster,
or for one of the actors to go insane,
like Anthony Hopkins, when he was playing Othello.
Did you hear about this? Way back in the Seventies.
He lost it, completely, right on stage.
He's right in the middle of this show, Othello,
and he tears off his make-up and starts talking to the
    audience.

DICK: Oh, right. I remember this now.
He wound up in the hospital right after that, didn't he?

NORM: I think so. Maybe. I'd have to look it up.
Anyway, the point is, imagine those people
sitting in that audience, watching Othello,
totally absorbed in that fictional world,
and then BOOM! The guy goes bull goose loony,
starts ranting hysterically, ripping off his black-face.

DICK: They probably thought it was part of the show.

NORM: At first, yeah. They would, naturally.

DICK:
Because they're so invested in the world of the play.

NORM: Right. I mean, the last thing you want
is to see this world, in which you've invested,
come grinding to a screeching halt
and fall to pieces right in front of your face.

DICK: This made-up world you chose to believe in.

NORM: And *were*, actually, believing in,
that is, until they blew it all up.

DICK: Wow, that would be so disorienting.
I mean, you wouldn't know where you were anymore.
What to believe. In which reality.

NORM: And *that*, Dick, is precisely the point.
That is exactly what they want.

DICK: The extremists?

NORM: Yes. These agitators.
These provocateurs and poetic terrorists.

DICK: So they want to destabilize how we think.
Subvert expectations. Play with our minds.

NORM: Exactly. See, they just bide their time,
waiting to pounce on the slightest slip up.
Take what happened, just now, for example.
What actually happened between you and me.
Now, if I was one of these poetic terrorists,
and you asked me what I was talking about,
like you did before, when we were talking about art,
or whatever the hell we were talking about,
now, I could've taken that moment of uncertainty,
that *rupture*, as they say, and run with it forever.
I could've taken us completely off-track
and down a blind alley that would lead us nowhere.
But I didn't do that. Did I, Dick?

DICK: No.

NORM: Why?

DICK: Because you're not an extremist?

NORM: That's right, Dick. And neither are you.
And because your viewers, and the American people,
or at least some vestige of the American people,
are expecting a serious discussion here,
of global politics, and the threats we're facing.
They watch this show because they want to be
    informed.
They want to get an inside political perspective,
on *politics*, and the *world*, that actually exists.

DICK: As opposed to our opinions on *art* or whatever.
I mean, what the hell do we know about art?
We're a couple of Washington insider types.

NORM: Right. Yes. That's who we are.

DICK: I mean, it's not like we're artists or art experts or
   anything.

NORM: They're two entirely different subjects.

DICK:
Which have nothing whatsoever to do with each other.

NORM: No. Right. And that's the point.
That's the big difference right there, Dick.
See, we're not up here to give a *performance*
and make fancy speeches and cloud the issues.
Now, I love a good speech as much as the next guy.
Plot. Characters. All that stuff.
People pretending to be other people.
Moving around. Making speeches.

DICK: In little imaginary made-up worlds.

NORM: Sure, that's great. I love that stuff.
But look, when you're into something like we are,
where *lives* and things like that are at stake,
when you're dealing with serious life-and-death issues,
man, I'll tell you, that is the last thing you want—

DICK: That's just bad politics, is what you're saying.

NORM: Politics? No. That's perfect politics.

DICK: But lousy theater.

NORM: Right. See,
in *politics*, yes, definitely, Dick,
you want fancy speeches. A lot of speeches.

DICK: And a big blatant message.

NORM: Sure. Hell,
it's not like you're working in nuances or anything.

DICK: You want to tell people what they want to hear
in exactly the way they're used to hearing it.

NORM: Keep your audience with you at all times.

DICK: Hook them at the outset. Tease them. Lead them.

NORM: Sometimes you do have to circle around,
or take a detour that doesn't lead anywhere,
to wind up back at the crux of a thing.
But that's all it is. A little detour.

DICK: Which brings you right back to reality. Right?

NORM: Reality. That's it. Common sense.

DICK: A re-presentation of what's real and true.

NORM: That reaffirms everything you already know.

DICK: Or think you know, or pretend to know.

NORM: And see, Dick, that is what sets us apart.
That's what we have that they do not.

DICK: What?

NORM: Honesty. Authenticity.
That's how we win the people's trust.
See, we don't have to play all these mind games, Dick,
twist reality all out of shape.
Because reality, and the truth, is on our side.
All we have to do is portray it,
present it to people, so they can recognize it.

DICK:
Whereas they have to call it into question all the time,
take it apart, de-construct it.

NORM: The extremists. Right. There you go, Dick.

DICK: So it's all about who controls ideas.

NORM: Ideas are capital. That's the key.

DICK: And the difference is, *our* ideas are *real*.
Whereas their ideas are just made-up concepts.

NORM: Fictions. They're just little imaginary worlds.

DICK: Which only exist so long as people believe—

NORM: That's all it really *is*, Dick,
a lot of people believing in things.

DICK: All believing in...the same thing.
Reinforcing each other's beliefs.

NORM: In essence, it's no different than what happens
  every day.
You turn the T V on. Flip through the channels.
There's Law and Order. Cops. Whatever.

DICK: The History Channel.

NORM: American Idol.

DICK: It all works together.

NORM: It's all connected.

DICK: That is the world. The fabric of the world.

NORM: Ideas. Images. Concepts. Beliefs.

DICK: But ours are real, and theirs aren't?

NORM: That's our advantage. That's why we'll win.

DICK:
So it all depends on how you take what you're hearing,
or seeing, or reading, as the case may be.

NORM: And who's behind it. Why it's there.
I mean, it's not there by accident.

DICK: Well, sometimes it is.
I mean, a television show? That you just stumbled on?

NORM:
Some random show that's just there by accident.

DICK:
That you're just kind of watching for no real reason.

NORM: Completely innocent. Not part of some scheme
to program your mind and control your thoughts.

DICK: Some shows are purely entertainment, right?

NORM: You think so, Dick? I think so too.
But you know what these radicals would say about
  that?

DICK: I think I can guess, but go ahead.

NORM: They'd tell you that even these innocent shows,
that are harmless entertainment and meaningless fun,
promote some particular view of the world.

DICK: What? A world of meaningless fun?

NORM: No, a world where everything, including fun,
entertainment, art, politics,
has all been reduced to its commodity value.

DICK: To products. For sale. Like tubes of toothpaste.

NORM: And not just art and philosophy, Dick,
healthcare, education, literature,
theater, spiritual practices even.

DICK: Sex. Romance.

NORM: Love itself.

DICK: Faith itself. Truth itself.

NORM: Truth. Love. Vacuum cleaners.

DICK: Liposuction. Absolution.

NORM: Fame. Respect. Fair-trade Kleenex.

DICK: Those little sweaters they make for dogs.

NORM: Friends. Ethics.

DICK: People's organs.
Livers. Kidneys. Eyes. Eggs.

NORM: People's brains.

DICK: Their minds, souls,
for sale, like products, like bars of soap.

NORM: This is the cynicism these people espouse.

DICK: The extremists.

NORM: And their cagey little cohorts, yes.

DICK: These saboteurs.

NORM: These infiltrators.

DICK:
Of course, they would never admit that, would they?

NORM: No. Of course not. If you ask them directly
they'll feed you some French post-structuralist hooey,
all this crap that no one understands,
how reality and truth are just made-up constructs,
games, signs, meaningless signs,
and the truth is that there *is* no truth,
no right or wrong, so anything goes.

DICK: Jesus.

NORM: Yeah. It's really insane.

DICK: It's like they want to get inside your mind.
Get directly inside your mind.

NORM: It's hardball, Dick. They're playing for keeps.

DICK: And what was it that sets us apart again?

NORM:
The fact that we don't have to hide what we're doing.

DICK: We don't?

NORM: No.

DICK: And what *are* we doing?

NORM: Programming minds.

DICK: Programming *minds*?

NORM: Or *de*-programming.

DICK: But that's what they're doing.

NORM: Right. Exactly.

DICK: Brainwashing people.

NORM: But see, Dick, we don't have to dance around it.
We can just come right out and say it.
"Here you go, folks. Here's the truth.
The truth as we see it. As science sees it.
As history sees it. See for yourselves."

DICK:
I'm sorry. Are you saying you're *for* brainwashing?

NORM:
When you're brainwashing people with the *truth*, sure.
I mean, we've all been trained, educated, right?
Taught how to read, to interpret the world.
How to behave. What to believe.
Who to obey, fear, respect.
Is that not implanting things in people's minds?

DICK:
So it's brainwashing either way, is what we're saying.

NORM: Pick your programming. Ours or theirs.

DICK:
So the choice is either be brainwashed with the *truth*,
or with a bunch of made-up extremist nonsense.

NORM: That's pretty much it in a nutshell, Dick.

DICK: But doesn't that kind of ruin everything?
I mean, knowing that you're being brainwashed and
  all?
Normally, you know, if you're going to be
  brainwashed,
you don't want to *know* that you're being brainwashed.

NORM: Actually, Dick, that's not really a problem.
Not anymore. It was in the past.
But people are pretty savvy these days.

DICK: Media savvy.

NORM: No question, Dick.
For example, we would never kid ourselves, would we,

that your viewers are going to mistake this exchange,
this conversation, that we're having right now,
for anything resembling a *real* conversation.

DICK: But it *is*, in fact, a real conversation.
Or an interview, rather, to be precise.

NORM: Big difference, Dick. World of difference.
And, Dick, I assure you, the average viewer,
someone watching this show right now,
can tell the difference between a *real* conversation
and one of these fake *T V* conversations.
And I'll tell you something else, Dick.
They know how to *read* these *T V* conversations,
you know, as opposed to a *real* conversation,
which you really don't have to read, do you?

DICK:
You mean, unless you're an extremist or something.

NORM: Right. But otherwise, with a *real* conversation,
you just have it, right? You just talk back and forth.
Like *real* people. On a *real* T V show.

DICK: It *is* a real show.

NORM: Of course it is.
It's completely real. All of this is.

DICK: It *is*.

NORM: I know. I just said that, Dick.

DICK: Look. OK. Programming. Fine.
Messaging. Ideology. Whatever.
People still need to know what to believe.
What's real and what's not. Don't they?

NORM: Sure.
If they didn't, hell, we'd be out of a job.

DICK: No one would take us seriously anymore.

NORM:
They'd see right through us. They'd laugh at us, Dick.

To them, we'd be no more than entertainment.
No different than actors or comedians or clowns.
Which, of course, is exactly what these people want.

DICK: The extremists.

NORM: Yes.

DICK: To make us look foolish.
Destroy our authority. Our credibility.

NORM: They want to destroy the people's trust.
They want to sow cynicism. Suspicion. Sarcasm.
Seduce the people with their pseudo-sincerity.
See, they're not blind. They see their opening.
They're going right after our Achilles Heel.

DICK: They know that people have lost their bearings.
That no-one understands the world anymore.
Who's running things. What's really going on.

NORM: Sure. Come on. Who's really in charge here?
Governments? Maybe. Corporations?
Cabals of unnamed corporate conspirators
hiding their holdings in the Cayman Islands?

DICK: The W E F? The W T O?

NORM: OPEC. ICANN. NAFTA. SAC.

DICK: I A E A. C D C.

NORM: FTSE. DAX. The D O D.

DICK: How are we supposed to keep it all straight?

NORM: We're not, Dick. That's the point.
It's gobbledygook. It's alphabet soup.

DICK: That only the prelacy is meant to understand.

NORM: The technocratic priesthood. Yes.

DICK: While the laity sits there, dumbfounded. Dazed.
Totally unable to even think anymore.
Their minds battered by this barrage of bullshit.

NORM: It's a carny trick, Dick. It's old as the hills.
First thing they do is, they get you lost,
totally confused, until your head is spinning,
and you don't know which way is up anymore—

DICK: And then they feed you some simplistic pseudo-
solution.

NORM: Which you swallow whole out of desperation.

DICK:
Out of frustration, because you don't understand.

NORM:
And you sense that you're not *going to* understand.

DICK: You're never *really* going to understand.
Are you? Ever?

NORM: No. You're not.

DICK: And so...what are we supposed to do?

NORM: Well, you either accept that or you don't.
Normally you do. Most people do.

DICK: And who can blame them?

NORM: Right. I mean,
normally, you're just trying to get through the day.
Get home. Eat. Watch T V.
What's real? Values? Who's really in charge?
Who has time for all these questions?

DICK: They're just distractions. A waste of time.

NORM: You get so lost in all this chaos,
trying to figure out what's going on,
and who's really running it, that you just shut down.

DICK:
Or you get so obsessed with trying to figure it all out,
analyzing everything till you're totally obsessed—

NORM: You can end up completely deranged, Dick,
reading messages into placemats in restaurants.

DICK: It's sad, isn't it, when you see people like that,
beaten down, their brains scrambled,
desperately trying to extract some point,
or anything even remotely intelligible,
from all the random nonsense coming at you.

NORM:
It's heartbreaking, Dick. It just breaks your heart.
It just breaks your heart into little pieces.

DICK:
You just want to cry when you see people like that.

NORM: You feel like there's this ocean of tears,
here in your heart. There's so much pain.

DICK: It feels like it's going to just break you in half
if you ever allow yourself to start to feel—

NORM: And right there, right at that vulnerable point,
is where the extremist enemy pounces.

DICK: Offering up some simplistic answer—

NORM: Usually it comes in the form of a question.

DICK: A question?

NORM: Yes. These people are pros.
They know exactly what they're doing, Dick.

DICK: What kind of a question?

NORM: A loaded question.

DICK:
Something that will get people questioning themselves,
questioning the way their minds are working,
the way their minds are programmed to work?

NORM: And what it is they really want.

DICK:
I suppose it always comes down to that, doesn't it?
I mean, what people *really* want.

NORM: And why they want it.

DICK: And why they can't have it.

NORM: Why they don't even *know* what they want.
Think about that. Ask yourself the question.
What do I want? Really want?

DICK: Sometimes that's a scary question.

NORM: This is how they work, Dick.
This is how they get into your mind.
They get you questioning your own desires.
Questioning your life, which is disappearing,
moment by moment. Now. Now.
Why aren't you doing exactly what you want?
Why don't you even know what you want?
What is wrong with you? What happened to you?

DICK: Hypothetically?

NORM: Of course. Yes.
I mean, nothing is really wrong, right?
You know what you want. You know what you're
   doing.

DICK: I think I do.

NORM: Of course you do.
You're a T V journalist. That's what you are.

DICK: O K. Sure—

NORM: That's your life.
That's what you've dedicated your life to, right?

DICK: Sure. Yeah. That's what I've chosen.

NORM: Chosen. Yes. There you go.
This is what you've *chosen* to do.
Therefore, this is what you *want*.
I mean, you wouldn't go and take up some profession,
that you didn't *care* about, deeply, would you?
You wouldn't do that, would you, Dick?

DICK: No. I guess not. What would be the *point*?

NORM: Why would you spend your entire *life*
at some boring job that didn't *mean* anything to you?

DICK: That wouldn't make much sense, would it?

NORM: No. Not much.

DICK: A waste of time.
A waste of one's *life*, really, when you think about it.

NORM: A completely meaningless waste of time.

DICK:
To just squander your life, like it was worth nothing.

NORM: Or to let it be squandered for you, by others.

DICK: To waste your life, being used by others,
who couldn't care less if you live or die,
passively playing a part in some system,
some system of *control* and *domination*
that sucks all the joy and meaning out of life.
The slave of some huge, invisible machine
that denies its very existence to your face,
that passes itself off as *reality* and *truth*,
and labels you insane if you ever start to question it,
if you ever even have the audacity to wonder,
why do things have to be this way?
Why do I have to live like this?
Why is my life was being wasted like this?
My one, fleeting life on this earth.
The one thing I have, that is mine alone.

NORM: Imagine...if you actually thought like that.

DICK: If you really felt like you were just a slave.

NORM: This is exactly how they make people feel.
They're very good. They know what they're doing.

DICK: Wow. You know, if that's how I felt,
how I really felt, I don't know what I'd do.

NORM: If you felt like your life was worth...nothing.
Like you were just some interchangeable drone,

pumped full of post-ideological programming
to keep you working and buying products.

DICK:
Might as well just kill yourself, and get it over with.

NORM: Or...even better, Dick,
why not just hurl yourself into the machinery.
I mean, once you realize you've got nothing to lose.
Better to die like a lion, right,
than live like a dog? Isn't that the saying?

DICK: *Sabotage* it. Attack from inside.

NORM: Like Samson in the temple. This is their logic.

DICK: The extremists.

NORM: Yes. These radicals, Dick.
Who spend all their time attacking the system—

DICK: O K, I think I'm getting this now.

NORM: See how they twist and contort people's minds?
They try to tap into our dissatisfaction.
Our disillusionment. Our broken dreams.

DICK: Everyone has them. We all do, don't we?
I mean, no-one sets out to become bitter,
to become some bitter backbiting cynic
who couldn't care less about his fellow man.

NORM: No, we start out with noble intentions.
Folks become lawyers so they can serve justice,
or politicians to serve their country,
or artists, writers, actors even.
They don't *set out* to prostitute themselves.
No, they fall in love with art,
literature, film, whatever it is,
and it's only later that they come to learn,
once they get into the system itself,
that it's just a front, and there's nothing there.

DICK: Nothing noble.

NORM: It's business. A game.

DICK: Who hasn't had their heart broken,
when they learned how what they loved most in life,
the thing they fell in love with as a child,
that to them was magic, and that became their life,
their life's work, all they cared about,
wound up just another power game,
a clutch of conniving sarcastic little sycophants
stabbing each other in the backs for status?

NORM: That's the pain they prey on, Dick.
They twist our grief into this violent rage.
This bitter, hopeless suicidal rage.
I mean, thank God that's not how we *really* feel, right?

DICK: Yeah. Thank God. I think I'd lose my mind.
I mean, I think I might go completely insane.
I'd probably become capable of...God, I don't know.
Horrible things. Anything really.

NORM: Who's to say how far you might go?

DICK: Luckily, that isn't how it *really* is.

NORM: In reality. No.

DICK: But Jesus. Wow.
It's so easy, isn't it, to start thinking that way.

NORM: Yes, it is. And they know this, Dick.
They know exactly what's in our hearts.
What's buried in there. Which buttons to press.

DICK: Anybody can look at freedom, democracy,
and focus on its flaws and shortcomings, right?
You can do that with anything, any ideal.
I mean, you've got the ideal, and then you've got the
  reality.

NORM: Look at the French and American Revolutions.

DICK: The Declaration of the Rights of Man.

NORM: The Bill of Rights. The Constitution.

64 THE EXTREMISTS

DICK: Individualism. Private property.

NORM: The rights of white male property owners.

DICK: Insurrection. The Reign of Terror.

NORM: Jefferson. Locke. Paine. Rousseau.

DICK: All the so-called Enlightenment philosophers.

NORM: You think this is what they had in mind?

DICK: No. Of course not. They wanted freedom.

NORM: Bad enough to actually *fight* for it, right?

DICK: Right. I mean, it was revolution.

NORM: Absolutely. It wasn't a game.

DICK: It wasn't some march, with signs and slogans.

NORM:
They *killed* the monarchy. They cut off their heads.

DICK: Happens in pretty much every revolution.

NORM: You don't make an omlette without breaking some eggs.

DICK: People don't just hand over power.

NORM:
No, you have to kill them, and take it from them.

DICK: Which, of course, they know you want to do.

NORM: Sure. On account of it's what they did.
I mean, that's what all the cops and soldiers are for.

DICK: To keep you from doing what they did to them.

NORM: Which of course...would be bad, and wrong.

DICK: Now that *they're* in charge, you mean.

NORM: Sure. I mean, say we did want to change things.

DICK: You and I?

NORM: And our viewers. Sure.

DICK: Like we wanted to overthrow the government or something?

NORM: Right. Just hypothetically, of course.

DICK:
Of course. That's the last thing we'd *really* want to do.

NORM: Right. But let's just *say* we did.
Now, we certainly wouldn't want to use violence or anything.

DICK: Absolutely not. It goes without saying.

NORM: No. We'd want to work *within* the system.

DICK: Influence people. Change people's minds.

NORM: Empower people. Enrich their minds.

DICK: Like with protest songs and all like that.

NORM: Stimulating arguments. Lively debate.

DICK: Poetry. Films. Theater even.

NORM: But never actual revolution.

DICK: No. Because that's all over now, right?
I mean, the *last* revolutions, that put *us* in charge,
they were necessary. We had no choice.
They were the oppressors. We had to kill them.
We had to slaughter them all like pigs.
But now, now that *we're* in charge,
it's all different. I mean, we're not like them.

NORM: No. Of course not. We're completely different.

DICK: I mean, nobody needs to slaughter *us*.

NORM: No, and anyone who thinks they do,
is clearly insane...dangerously insane.

DICK: Which is what the monarchy said about us.

NORM: Right.

DICK: And what we're saying...now.

NORM: No. That's what *they're* saying, Dick.

DICK: Who? The monarchy?

NORM: No. They're dead.

DICK: We killed them all, right?

NORM: Yes, we did.

DICK: So that's what *who's* saying?

NORM: The extremists, Dick.
That's what these terrorists want to get us to believe.

DICK: So that we'll question ourselves and doubt our
own values.

NORM: So that we'll doubt them to the point that we
  begin to believe
that it was *all* about power, all along.

DICK: That all our talk of freedom and justice
was just a smoke screen, empty words.

NORM: A new form of power talking to itself,
about itself, justifying itself.

DICK: That the thing we're fighting so hard to defend,
to keep alive, was never alive.

NORM: It was always just this simulation,
this mockery, of what we really want.

DICK: Something stillborn.

NORM: A wicker man.

DICK: Jesus, this is really sinister.

NORM: That's right, Dick. That's exactly what it is.
Sinister. Evil. There's no other word.
Twisting well-meaning people's minds
until they can't tell black from white anymore
and they're ready to turn against their own culture,
their own people. It's evil. It's sick.

DICK: But, of course, they wouldn't say it that way.

NORM:
No. They'd tell you they were fighting for freedom.
They call themselves anti-authoritarians.
As if they were fighting all forms of tyranny.

DICK: But they're not.

NORM: No. They're nihilists, Dick.
They believe in nothing. They're weak. Sick.
All they want us to do, really,
is die, surrender, self-destruct.

DICK: Like Anthony Hopkins playing Othello.

NORM: Actually, it might have been the Scottish play.

DICK: But then, why would he be wearing black-face?

NORM: Right. Good point. Look, it doesn't matter.
What matters is...it wasn't him.

DICK: It wasn't Anthony Hopkins?

NORM: No.
Yes. I mean, it *was* Anthony Hopkins,
or Richard Harris, or one of those guys.

DICK: Richard Burton?

NORM: Whoever. Look,
whoever it was, it wasn't *really* him.
It was just his *disease*, his broken mind.

DICK: He's an alcoholic.

NORM: A drunk. Yes.
I mean, he's all better now. He's rich and famous.

DICK: You're saying his disease is what made him do it.

NORM:
It warped his mind, Dick, the way he saw things,
until everything looked so ugly and hollow
and vain that he actually ruined his own *show*!

DICK: Why would anyone in his right mind do that?

NORM: Exactly, Dick. Why would you do that?

DICK: Attack the very thing that supports you.

NORM: The thing you've dedicated your entire life to.

DICK: You wouldn't, would you? Unless you were sick.

NORM:
Or unless you believed that what you were doing,
was so pointless and empty and utterly meaningless—

DICK: Unless you believed it was already dead.

NORM: Or, worse than dead, in some *vegetative state*.

DICK: Like a patient in a hospital, whose brain is dead.

NORM: A pathetic, empty simulation of itself.

DICK: Being kept alive with expensive machines.

NORM: A mockery of some forgotten ritual.

DICK: Everything shiny and clean and sterile.

NORM: The visitors sitting there, looking on.
At visiting hour. Pretending to visit.

DICK: Fewer and fewer as the years wear on.

NORM: Visiting purely out of duty or habit.
Not the vaguest memory of what the point
of the exercise could have possibly been.

DICK: And then in walks Richard Harris or whoever,
goes over to the machine and just pulls the plug.

NORM: Starts asking people, is *this* what you want?
What do you want? Why are you here?

DICK: Poor delusional drunken bastard.

NORM: Actually asking people what they want.

DICK: Why they're doing what they're doing.

NORM: Why they're living the way they're living.
Putting up with what they're putting up with.

DICK:
As if he was actually going to change their minds.
Or change the world.

NORM: Or the theater even.

DICK: Man, good thing he got into recovery.
He's fine now, right?

NORM: Yeah, he's completely normal.
He'd never do anything like that these days.

DICK: Ruin a show.

NORM: Subvert the system.

DICK: Sow instability.

NORM: Insurrection.

DICK: Try to get in there and mess with people's minds.

NORM:
Get right in there and disrupt the programming.

DICK:
Imagine the arrogance. Believing you could do that.

NORM: See, Dick? This is how they've got us thinking.

DICK: The extremists.

NORM: Yes. See, they've warped our minds.
They've got us believing that *anything* is possible.

DICK: That we could actually affect people's lives.

NORM: With art. Theater.

DICK: It's just entertainment.
I mean, where did we ever get this idea
that we could somehow change the world?
Or that it even *needs* changing?

NORM: They've gotten right into our heads, Dick.
They've infected us all with this radical doubt.
They've got us doubting, well...everything, really.
Everything we say. Everything we think.

DICK: We don't even know who we are anymore.

NORM:
We're like actors in a play that we no longer believe in.
We're saying our lines. We're hitting our marks.
But it all feels empty and fake and wrong.
Sure, we deny it, as best we can.
We distract ourselves with T V, drugs,
sex, whatever...but we *all* feel it.
We *all* know it's there. Here. Always.

DICK: This sense that something has come to an end.

NORM: Our *world*, Dick. The world we knew.

DICK: It's like the apocalypse had already happened
and we're in some state of suspended animation.

NORM: That's it, Dick. That's it exactly.
That is exactly how they want us to feel.

DICK: Like it's already over. And we're just stringing
things out.

NORM: Even though we all know what needs to
happen.

DICK: You mean pull the plug.

NORM: And just walk out.

DICK: Out...of what?

NORM: Out of the *hospital*.

DICK: And how did we get into the hospital again?

NORM:
We didn't. That's just what they want us to believe.

DICK: That we're in a hospital?

NORM: That this is how we think.

DICK: Then we're *not* in a hospital.

NORM: No. We're here.

DICK: Here. On television.

NORM: Sure, if you like.

DICK: And if I don't?

NORM: It doesn't matter.

DICK: I have no idea what we're saying now.

NORM: We *are*...wherever we *believe* we are,
doing whatever we *believe* we're doing.

DICK: According to them.

NORM: These lunatics, yes.
See, they want us to believe that none of this is real.
That it's all made-up...just signs and words,
which conjure a world, a conceptual model—

DICK: Which looks like a hospital?

NORM: No, which looks like *reality*.

DICK: But isn't real?

NORM: No, it's completely real.
It's the world itself...reality itself.

DICK: I thought we just said it was all made-up.

NORM: Right. Exactly.

DICK: It's all a myth,
a story that power is telling itself.

NORM: The one it's been telling itself all along.

DICK: Like looking in a mirror and talking to yourself.
Telling yourself you're brave and strong.

NORM: Therefore your enemy has to be weak.

DICK: Cowardly. Evil.

NORM: Sick. Wrong.

DICK: So it's really just all about morality then.

NORM: Morality? Don't be ridiculous. No.
Nobody's had any morals for years.
Centuries, actually, truth be told.

It's all about whether you're *normal* now.
Whether you conform—

DICK: To the model.

NORM: Right.

DICK: Some mythical norm, some ideal state—

NORM: Which can never be attained and in relation to which
everything and everyone is constantly measured.

DICK:
So that even when someone is completely healthy,
that's just one degree of being sick.

NORM: Like good was always just a measure of evil.
When the myth was moral, instead of scientific.

DICK: The myth?

NORM: The truth.

DICK: What's real.

NORM: Right.

DICK: Wait. What's real? What's true? Or the myth?

NORM: What's the difference?

DICK: That's what I'm asking.

NORM: Look, Dick, if we see the world one way,
if we all believe that's where we are,
more or less, and we *behave* that way,
like we're in that place, then that's where we are.

DICK: And if we all believe we're somewhere else,
then *that's* where we are?

NORM: Pretty much. Yeah.

DICK: That's magical thinking.

NORM: Absolutely.

DICK:
You're saying, for example, that when people believed
that our bodies were composed of of biles and humors
instead of cells and genes and whatever,
because that's what everyone believed at the time,
that our bodies *were* made of biles and humors?

NORM:
And when a doctor bled somebody with leeches—

DICK: What? They recovered?

NORM: Yes. They did.

DICK: And so, by extension, when we all believed
that our dreams were messages from angels and
   demons,
because that's what we *all* believed—

NORM: That's what they were.

DICK: And so, *now,*
because we believe they're repressed desires,
like Freud proposed—

NORM: That's what they are.

DICK: And if I disagree?

NORM: Well, then you're insane.
You've probably got some kind of chemical imbalance.
But hey, don't worry. We've got all kinds of medicines,
drugs and things, to fix you right up.

DICK: To make me *normal.*

NORM: Like the rest of us. Yeah.

DICK: To eliminate any deviation from the norm,
make sure that everyone and everything conforms
to the rules of *reality*...which do not exist.

NORM: Sure. But listen, it's for your own good.
I mean, we just want everyone to be healthy and
   happy.

Oh, and we need to make *sure* that you're healthy and
happy.
So we need to check you. See how you're doing.
We need to check you constantly, in fact.
And we need you to check yourself constantly.
Make sure you're thinking healthy thoughts.

DICK: Wait. Hold on now. Who needs to check?
We need to check? *They* need to check?

NORM: Everyone. Everybody needs to check.

DICK: No, I meant, according to who?

NORM: What?

DICK: Us, or the extremists, or who?

NORM: Who what?

DICK: Who is *saying* this?
Is this *us* saying this? Or is this...us
saying what they say we say they say?

NORM: Exactly, Dick. Who can tell anymore?
Who can tell who's saying what?
Or doing what. Or what's going on.

DICK: O K. Right. But we're still us.

NORM: Are we?

DICK: Yes. I mean, I'm *me*.
This is me talking.

NORM: Is it? You're sure?
These are your thoughts? These are your words?

DICK: Yes. I mean, I'm *saying* them, aren't I?

NORM: Absolutely. You're not some robot.

DICK: No. I'm not.

NORM: No. Right.
It's not like you're programmed or anything like that,
like you'd assumed some role or adopted some model

of the person you always wanted to be,
or were *told* that you were *supposed* to be,
and molded yourself to match that appearance.

DICK: No.

NORM: No. Right. You're you.
An authentic person. A real person.
You're not some spy. Impersonating yourself.
Wearing a mask. A Dick Hedgerow mask.
Some infiltrator. Pretending. Faking.
Waiting, patiently, for your chance to pounce,
to release some perceptual virus into the Real,
some kind of insidious mimetic code,
to subvert reality and scramble our brains.

DICK: You're not, actually—

NORM: Of course not, Dick.
All I'm saying is, if you *were* some spy,
some sneaky saboteur, sowing discontent
and rebellion and paranoia everywhere—

DICK: Which I'm not.

NORM: I know. That's not what we're saying.

DICK: Well, what are we saying?

NORM: Nothing.

DICK: Nothing?

NORM:
We're not saying anything. We're *doing* something.

DICK: Alright. Fine. Then what are we doing?

NORM: According to who?

DICK: According to us.

NORM: Nothing.

DICK: Nothing?

NORM: No. Of course not.
Nothing is actually happening here.

DICK: It isn't?

NORM: No. It's just a show.

DICK: So we're not really doing anything.

NORM: Unless, that is—

DICK: We *aren't* us.

NORM: Right.

DICK: Which...would make us *them*.

NORM: Right.

DICK: The extremists. Which...we're not.

NORM: Unless we're lying.

DICK: Which we could be, right?

NORM: Right.

DICK: I mean, how could you be sure?

NORM: You couldn't.

DICK: Not if we were any good.

NORM: And in any event, you couldn't prove it.

DICK: No. We'd just deny it, wouldn't we?

NORM: Sure. We'd just deny it to your face.
What are you going to do, arrest us?

DICK: Wow. Man. That would be weird.
That would be so confusing, wouldn't it?
There we'd be, standing right there,
right there in the flesh, like we are right now—

NORM: Right there on your little *screen*.

DICK: Impersonating real-life television people.

NORM: Pumping out our perceptual virus.

DICK: Desperately trying to jam our signal.

NORM: Hack the system.

DICK: Screw with your head.

NORM: Get you to see the machine at work.

DICK: Talking to itself inside your head.

NORM: See, we need to inoculate against that, Dick.
We need to get in there, inside people's heads,
and take some goddamn pre-emptive measures.

DICK: So that should that ever actually happen,
if these infiltrators ever actually got in there,
and started screwing around inside your head—

NORM: Right. It wouldn't matter, see?

DICK: Because we'd have gotten in there first.

NORM: And inoculated. Absolutely.

DICK:
So that even if they managed to get in there somehow,
through some sneaky surreptitious subterfuge,
nothing they said would have any effect.

NORM: It couldn't touch you. You'd be immune.

DICK: You probably wouldn't even understand it.
You wouldn't even recognize what they were doing.

NORM: It would be like listening to some crazy person
babbling paranoid nonsense on the street.

DICK: You'd dismiss it instinctively, without a thought.

NORM:
Your mind would be sealed. There'd be no way in.

DICK: Hermetically sealed.

NORM: Quarantined off.

DICK:
You'd just look at them and shake your head, sadly.

NORM: And take your remote and just click them off.

DICK: Click them away...into outer space.

NORM: Click them away...like it never happened.

DICK:
And go back to whatever the hell you were doing.

NORM: And how you were thinking.

DICK: To your normal life.

NORM: Where you understand what everything is.

DICK: And how it all works.

NORM: And can follow the rules.

DICK: And can follow the story.

NORM: Yeah, it's not too hard,
considering it's always the same story.

DICK: Telling you, "this is the way it is."

NORM: And always was, and always will be.

DICK: Look...here's a reflection of it.
It's *real*. It's *true*. It's the way life is.
It's not a reflection of some made-up reality,
programming your mind with its latent logic.

NORM: No. It's art. It's self-expression.
Some artist held a mirror up to the world.

DICK: The *real* world, which actually exists.
Not just an effect. A simulation.

NORM: No. The made-up *story* is the reflection.
The *world*, the thing reflected, is real.

DICK: It's all just a question of interpretation.

NORM: That's all it is. It's not *creation*.
It's not like we're, you know, making it all up,
like we're creating...reality...out of thin air, basically.

DICK: And nothing were really real...or true.

NORM:
And reality was just what we could get you to believe.

DICK: Or what somebody else could get you to believe.

NORM: Could get the majority of people to believe.

DICK: No. That's nuts. That's crazy. Right?

NORM: Of course. I mean, just imagine, for a minute. Imagine...if we had that kind of power.

END OF PLAY